SEEK
FOR
GLORY

PRAYING THE
PRAYER OF JABEZ

Bob Perry & Amy Joy Lykosh

MAKARIOS
PRESS

Esmont, VA

Makarios Press
P.O. Box 28, Esmont, VA 22937

Scripture in NIV unless otherwise stated.

Cover: Nate Braxton
Design: Nate Braxton

ISBN 978-1-956561-19-7

Printed in the United States of America

A Breakthrough Prayer

I thank you, Lord God, that you are known by many names. I thank you that you are known by Jehovah-Jireh, "the God who provides"; and Jehovah-Rapha, "the God who heals"; and Jehovah-Nisi, "our God, our covering, our banner, our protection."

But Lord, I feel like in this season, what I really want, Lord God, is to know you as the God of the breakthrough.

I want that God who's going to come into the midst of my mess, and, like a mighty flood, sweep away the resistance.

So, Lord God, I ask that your people would have the breakthroughs that they need.

Lord God, I speak that you are the Baal-perazim, the God of the breakthrough, the master of breakthroughs.

Lord God, rain down your breakthrough on your brothers and sisters, on your children, this week.

In the name of Jesus, please do this. Amen.

CONTENTS

INTRODUCTION

At one point, Bob said:

You know, Amy ... the prayer of Jabez is really suited to what we carry.

We carry a heart to bless.

We carry a desire for greatness.

We don't want to go along, mindlessly, with the culture, but, like Jabez, a standout in his generation, we want to be standouts, too.

We, too, want to be people of prayer and blessing.

We seek to be strategic, and to build God's kingdom.

When we pray, we expect that what we ask for, God provides.

And it's not because we've had every single wish and desire of our lives satisfied. Neither of us are billionaires, and we've both had pretty significant financial challenges at different times. But we still pray in faith, because God is faithful.

Bob Perry's Backstory

In January 1983, Bob, as a young man and a several-year-old believer, was at a prayer meeting.

Visiting evangelist and prophet Dick Mills looked at him and said, "Young man, I think you are a person of prayer. And I have a prayer for you. If you will pray I Chronicles 4:10 every day for the rest of your life, this is going to be a powerful prayer for you."

Bob began praying that prayer then, and he continues to pray it to this day.

Seventeen years after this conversation, the runaway bestseller *The Prayer of Jabez* came out.

In 2000, Bob was a missionary, church planter, and prayer leader in Eastern Europe.

When he read Wilkinson's book, he found that he experienced a real upgrade of praying for breakthrough.

This book includes his thoughts and insights, after about four decades of praying the same verse.

Amy Joy's Backstory

As a book reviewer of several decades, I refused to read *The Prayer of Jabez* for more than twenty years.

But when Bob, as my prayer mentor, prayed it over me, and taught it to me, I was taken aback by its beauty and its power.

Gobsmacked, really.

Apparently sometimes things are popular for a reason.

This book includes my research and deep dives into the language and meaning.

I wrote the words, so all the first person stories are mine. Bob, as mentor, teacher, prayer cover, and friend, offered input and direction, and many of the prayers are his. This is, truly a joint effort.

We offer this prayer to you as a special treat from the scripture.

We invite you to receive this gift: to celebrate, to enjoy, and to return to as a continual feast.

PROLOGUE
Why this prayer matters

You probably have heard some of the names of God.

El Shaddai: Lord God Almighty.

Jehovah Rapha: The Lord that heals.

Adonai: Master, Lord.

But a lesser-known name is this: "Baal-perazim," "the God of the breakthroughs."

Or, in different translation, "the owner of breakings through," or "the master of breakthroughs."

In II Samuel 5, we read about David, who faced a major problem.

He didn't want to lose to the Philistines, but he didn't know how to fight.

When he asked God, the Lord gave him a strategy.

"And David came to Baal-perazim, and David defeated them there. And he said, 'The LORD has broken through my enemies before me like a breaking flood.' Therefore the name of that place is called Baal-perazim" (II Samuel 5:20).

David came to a place whose name was "master of breakthroughs," and there he had a breakthrough.

The God of the breakthrough fought for him.

Later in this chapter, David had other battles with the Philistines.

Scripture says that he inquired of the Lord, and the God of
the breakthrough showed him what to do.

Through the various plans God gave him, David won the
victory because the Lord broke through.

When Bob read the story of Jabez, he was in the small
nation of Latvia, hidden from the mainstream.

He wasn't in Western Europe. Not in China. Not New York
or Washington, DC or Chicago or Los Angeles.

But when he read about Jabez, he thought, "If I'll pray
this prayer, giants will fall. If I pray this prayer of Jabez,
breakthrough will come. If I pray this prayer, my narrative
will change."

When he read about Jabez, he realized that God doesn't act
based on your pedigree, or your parents, or your position.

Rather, we simply need to understand who we want to
be (or, perhaps, who we are called to be), and ask God for
our identity.

Bob wondered, "What was I hoping for? Was I content to let
circumstances and situations put me in a box? Or was I going
to cry out to God through this simple prayer, this simple,
believing prayer, and trust the Lord, that he was going to
rewrite my narrative, trust the Lord that he was going to do
great things?"

Monday through Friday, he and others would spend an
hour each morning praying this prayer. He would choose
one part of the prayer as the focus, and then pray through it
extensively.

The prayer of Jabez made him want to live large for God.

*I wanted to believe for the touch of greatness, the dream to impact
and influence others, even though my circumstances said "No way."*

*And when I looked at Jabez, here's a man whose mother had
named him Pain. In the Hebrew culture, a good name was better
than gold or silver; a name speaks your destiny; a name speaks to
your course, your purpose, what you will do.*

A name has a lot of power, what you speak over people.

Jabez didn't let his name frame him in terms of disappointment or limits.

You could feel the heart of legacy. You could feel the desire in him to live beyond the limits, to break through the ceiling, to destroy the giants.

When I prayed this, I could see how powerful it is to pray this prayer and believe that God would bring a blessing.

Why not believe? Why not ask?

Our God becomes our victory.

At times, take a holy pause and pray over your work.

You speak this prayer and declare that the Lord is going to bless the territory at your job. He's going to bless the territory of your entrepreneur gift. He's going to bless the territory of your leadership, your company, giving you wisdom, giving you knowledge, giving you ideas, giving you vision, giving you favor. That's important, to ask the Lord to bless you and what you have in your hand and enlarge your border to increase the influence and impact.

Have you asked the Lord that he would bless your business with wisdom? That he'd give keen marketing principles and abilities to solve any problem?

The Lord wants us to build a legacy.

BACKGROUND

In the Midst of the Genealogy

A hidden treasure

In the Old Testament, the majority of the first fifteen chapters of the book of I Chronicles is an extended genealogy.

Beginning with Adam, the list runs through various family lines, including Israel, Caleb, David, Judah, Saul.

Fifteen chapters of verses like 6:10, "And Johanan begat Azariah (he it is that executed the priest's office in the temple that Solomon built in Jerusalem)."

You can find lists of David's mighty men, of the men who helped David become king, and of the people who worshiped as David brought the ark of the covenant to Jerusalem.

At best, you might recognize a few names. Most of the five hundred or so people lived and died in relative obscurity.

For a historian, presumably this list offers a goldmine of information.

But for the casual reader, it's not the most exciting.

And for the poor individual asked to read a chapter aloud in a group setting?

Absolute torture, for both reader and listener.

And yet, in the midst of page after page of names, chapter four has this unexpected treasure.

Jabez was more honorable than his brothers. His mother had named him Jabez, saying, "I gave birth to him in pain."

Jabez cried out to the God of Israel, "Oh, that you would bless me and enlarge my territory! Let your hand be with me, and keep me from harm so that I will be free from pain." And God granted his request. (I Chronicles 4:9-10 NIV)

The Message records the story like this:

Jabez was a better man than his brothers, a man of honor. His mother had named him Jabez (Oh, the pain!), saying, "A painful birth! I bore him in great pain!" Jabez prayed to the God of Israel: "Bless me, O bless me! Give me land, large tracts of land. And provide your personal protection—don't let evil hurt me." God gave him what he asked.

Why would the author call out this one man?

It's a great story!

Come on!

On Being Honorable

Jabez was more honorable than his brothers

In that culture, at that time, "brothers" did not necessarily mean literal brothers-born-from-the-same-mother.

Though the word could be literal brothers, it could also be kindred.

This sentence means, "Jabez was more honorable than his family and his *kindred.*"

Those words "more honorable"—an interesting choice of words.

Among 26 translations, 18 of them translate that phrase as "more honorable."

Another four are similar: *more honored, enjoyed more honor,* or, for two, *is honored.*

One said *more famous,* and three used the words *most respected.*

Honorable means *eminence and distinction, worthy of high respect and esteem.*

The Hebrew word agrees with that definition.

But it also means:

Heavy.

Weighty.

Grievous.

Hard.

Rich.

Glorious.

There's heft to this word.

In a community of changeable men and superficial beliefs, Jabez was more focused, more dedicated, more grounded.

But based on his given name, that's not what we would expect.

His Name

Difficult hardship

His mother had named him Jabez, saying,
"I gave birth to him in pain"

I realize that occasionally the Lord grants a birth
without pain.

But most women, from the time of Eve, experience at least
some pain with labor and delivery.

So why would Jabez's mother say, "I gave birth to him
in pain"?

It seems like a truism.

Presumably her pain was beyond the normal experience.

Perhaps the labor and delivery caused a fourth degree
perineal tear between her vaginal opening and her anus.

Pause a moment and consider: today, in the first world,
modern obstetrics makes such tears almost a non-issue. A
surgeon repairs the damage and the woman goes home sore,
but with a baby and a restored body.

In the third world, though, even today, such tears
completely destroy a woman's life.

Imagine expecting to have a baby, and ending up with
permanent anal incontinence.

Thank you, God, for all who serve in obstetrics. We ask your grace
for this hurting world.

"I gave birth to him in pain."

Or perhaps this mother was grieving a situation in her
life at the time of the birth. Death of a husband, death of a

beloved family member.

No definite answers here.

Jabez came into the world.

His mother gave birth to him in pain.

And so gave him a name that reflected her life.

Jabez means *pain,* or *difficult hardship.*

Another, even worse translation: *he makes sorrowful.*

In Russian, this name is *Trudna,* which means, *hard, with no hope,* or *difficulty and hardship with no promise at the end of the rainbow.*

Every time someone called the name *Jabez,* they spoke of hopelessness and hardship.

But it's worse than that.

On Being Cursed

A name, a destiny, a purpose

In the West today, a child's name might mean something ... but it also might not.

Isaiah Jude, for example: a beautiful name that means "Yahweh is salvation; he is exalted."

Or *Rosemary Grace*: "Remember grace."

But some parents choose a name simply because they like how it sounds.

Avery: a beautiful name that means "ruler of the elves."

Or *Natalia*: a beautiful name that means "Christmas day." (Though not all Natalias are born on Christmas day, may they all celebrate the nativity of Christ.)

That's the West today.

In the East, in the Hebrew culture at the time of Jabez, a name was different.

A person's name brought identity.

The name brought purpose.

The name even brought destiny.

A person's name not only defined them, but called out who they would become.

Thus, God renamed the man known as "Abram," or "exalted father." He became "Abraham," or "father of a multitude," or "father of nations."

Every time Abraham heard his name, he was hearing his destiny.

Jabez, clearly, did not have a positive name.

To say, "Good morning, Jabez," was actually saying, "Good morning, Pain. Good morning, Sorrow. Good morning, Hardship. Good morning, Defeat. Good morning, Disappointment."

Not just enervating words.

But his destiny, spoken again and again.

Defeat, failure, pain.

And Yet ...

More honorable

Though Jabez's name gave him no right to hope—indeed, removed hope—he was more honorable than his brothers.

How hard won was this weighty, glorious esteem?

How costly?

We don't know how much he struggled with insecurity, how much failure he wrestled through.

We just know that, despite his name, he was preeminent and respected among his kindred.

Oh, what a commendation!

And how beautiful, to realize that no matter what our name is, whether it suits us precisely, or we find ourselves fighting against it, we can choose an identity that aligns with God and with our destiny.

The Prayer

In its entirety

Jabez cried out to the God of Israel, "Oh, that you would bless me and enlarge my territory! Let your hand be with me, and keep me from harm so that I will be free from pain." And God granted his request.

Jabez offers a four part prayer, a bold prayer. He asked God for four things.

1. Bless me.
2. Enlarge my territory.
3. Let your hand be with me.
4. Keep me from harm that I will be free from pain.

And the scripture says: God granted his request.

Let's examine this amazing prayer in depth.

The Beginning

Jabez cried out

Do you picture this as a mellow prayer?

As a calm, dispassionate request?

Wrong!

Jabez *cried out*!

Some other possible translations: he *called out, uttered a loud sound, cried for help.*

Bob describes this more like a pounding on the table prayer: "I'm not letting up until I see a breakthrough!"

Does this seem a bit extreme?

It shouldn't.

When we get a breakthrough, our breakthrough blesses others.

When Thomas Edison got his breakthrough in lighting, his breakthrough changed the world.

When William Wilberforce got his breakthrough in England, enslaved people worldwide shared his triumph as they went free.

One person's breakthrough can shift daily life and the history of the nations of the earth.

It's good to pound the table.

Because the world still awaits breakthrough in many places.

The One Addressed

To the God of Israel

When Jabez prayed, he prayed to the God of Israel.

This God goes by many names. Some scholars have counted over 100.

Since we know that names offer identity, let's look at some of the names of God.

The scripture offers five specific compound names of God that help to define who he is.

Numerous other scriptures include the name "Jehovah" and another descriptive term, such as Psalm 23:1, where we read that "Jehovah" is "our shepherd."

But these five, in the Hebrew, smoosh the words together, so that they are uniquely crafted.

Each of these five compound names begin with the name "Jehovah," which means "our God, our great supreme ruler." Think of God's supremacy, his rulership, his authority.

And then the second part of the compound name is what God has done for us.

So the pattern is: "Supreme Ruler + benefit."

In order by appearance in the scriptures:

Jehovah-jireh.

In one of the most unexpected stories of the Old Testament, God tells his friend Abraham to sacrifice his son Isaac, child of promise.

When Abraham goes to do what God said, the LORD provides a ram and the son lives.

"So Abraham called that place The LORD Will Provide [Jehovah-jireh]. And to this day it is said, 'On the mountain of the LORD it will be provided'."[1]

God will see to it.

The God who sees.

God's provision shall be seen.

Jehovah-nissi.

The children of Israel faced the Amalek, their enemies. Joshua went out to fight, and Moses, the man of God, held up his hands.

With his hands up, the Israelites had the upper hand.

But he grew weary—fighting against gravity is no joke—so Aaron and Hur brought a stone for him to sit on, and they stood and supported Moses' arms, until the children of Israel won the victory.

"Moses built an altar and called it The LORD is my Banner [Jehovah-nissi]."[2]

God is our banner, our protection, our victory.

The word "nissi" is a military banner, the banner lifted up, the standard, the signal, the ensign, the sign, the rallying point.

The Great Supreme Ruler gives us victory.

Jehovah-shalom.

Once the Israelites settled in the Promised Land, they regularly forgot the LORD.

When they did, he gave them over to oppressors.

At one point, they were oppressed by the Midianites.

After seven years of severe treatment, they cried out to the LORD.

And so the angel of the LORD came to Gideon, to call him to lead.

This interaction was intense and fiery, until Gideon feared for his life.

"But the LORD said to him, 'Peace! Do not be afraid. You are not going to die.'

"So Gideon built an altar to the LORD there and called it The LORD Is Peace [Jehovah-shalom]. To this day it stands in Ophrah of the Abiezrites."[3]

God is peace.

In English, *peace* means either *absence of war* or, at times, *freedom from disturbance, tranquility.*

But the Hebrew word for peace, *shalom*, is far more rich in meaning. The Bible dictionary defines it as including both the English meanings, but also:

Completeness in number.

Safety and soundness in body.

Welfare, health, prosperity.

Quiet, contentment.

Peace, friendship of human relationships, and with God in covenant relationship.

Another way to describe it would be: *right relationships between God and man, man and man, man and self, man and nature.*

All-encompassing a well-being.

That's our God.

Jehovah-shalom.

Jehovah-tsidkenu.

Jeremiah, called "The Weeping Prophet," author of the book
that bears his name and the book of Lamentations, gives
a beautiful prophecy in Jeremiah 23. He writes about the
overthrow of the wicked shepherds, and the restoration that
is coming.

"The days are coming," declares the LORD,
"when I will raise up for David a righteous Branch,
a King who will reign wisely
and do what is just and right in the land.
In his days Judah will be saved
and Israel will live in safety.
This is the name by which he will be called:
The LORD Our Righteous Savior [Jehovah-tsidkenu].[4]

Jeremiah returns to this theme again in chapter 33.
In the midst of the desolate waste, in the midst of the
devastated land:

"'The days are coming,' declares the LORD, 'when I will fulfill the
good promise I made to the people of Israel and Judah.
"'In those days and at that time
I will make a righteous Branch sprout from David's line;
he will do what is just and right in the land.
In those days Judah will be saved
and Jerusalem will live in safety.
This is the name by which it will be called:
The LORD Our Righteous Savior [Jehovah-tsidkenu].'"[5]

God our righteousness.
Restored to God.

Jehovah-shammah.

Ezekiel, one of the most mystical (and, thus, difficult to understand) prophets, has an extended prophetic word about how the Jewish exile will end, and the city will be rebuilt.

The book of Ezekiel ends with these words:

"And the name of the city from that time on will be: the LORD is there [Jehovah-shammah]."[6]

God is there.

The last compound name of God before the 400 years of silence.

The last compound name of God before the coming of Jesus, the God who, indeed, is there.

How to Pray the Names of God

Creative thinking

When Bob would pray this prayer for an hour, he would begin with worship, praising the name of our God.

Like Jabez, he wanted to acknowledge the God of Israel, the one he was praying to.

Like Jesus, who taught his followers to pray, "Hallowed by *thy name.*"

Jehovah, supreme ruler and authority.

The LORD will provide.

The LORD our banner.

The LORD our peace.

The LORD our righteous savior.

The LORD is there.

Beautiful names of God.

But when Bob would pray, he didn't stop with these five names, nor even additional names like *Jehovah m'kaddesh*, the God who sanctifies; *Jehovah rophe*, the God who heals; *Jehovah rohi*, the Lord my shepherd.

In fact, he shocked me when he said, "David called God 'shepherd' out of his own experience. As a shepherd, he could see how God was a shepherd. It's okay to use your own life as a way to praise God. The Hebrew compound names for God came about because of the victory and breakthrough experiences of the Hebrew people. They were personal names."

Which is to say: yes, celebrate the names of God in the scripture, but also invite God into your own life experience as well.

As a prayer person, Bob asks Jesus, the great intercessor, "Oh, Jesus! Teach me to pray more effectively!"

And, yes, he can claim that from verses like Romans 8:34, "Christ Jesus who died—more than that, who was raised to life—is at the right hand of God and is also interceding for us," and Hebrews 7:25, "Therefore he is able to save completely those who come to God through him, because he always lives to intercede for them."

But if you think about it, Jesus was also the teacher. He was a craftsman and small businessman. He was a preacher, a healer. He knew about commerce and taxes and government. He had a family of origin.

He understands what it is to be a man.

So as a writer, I could pray, "God, you are the great storyteller, who writes beautiful stories of redemption in my life and the lives of those around me. Please write through me this day."

God is a personal God, and we can pray names for him from our experiences.

THE FIRST REQUEST

A Big Ask

Oh, that you would bless me

If only You would bless me
Oh, that You would bless me indeed
Oh that You would greatly bless me
Please bless me
Bless me, God
Please bless me
Whether you would bless me again and again
If only you would greatly bless me[7]

What Is a Blessing?

By definition

"To bless" is to ask for divine favor upon someone, to ask God to look favorably on a person.

The Hebrew word for bless, *barak*, means:

Abundantly
Adore
Altogether
Be blessed
Bless
Congratulate
Greatly
Kneel
Praise
Salute
Thank

Get Everything You Can

Is this really as good as it gets?

Here's the most mind-bending part of praying a blessing: it accomplishes something.

When we ask God to bless others and ourselves, we are asking for more.

Which means: if we don't ask, we don't get all that God has for us.

Does this leave you gasping?

It should.

Because if you don't ask for the blessing, you miss out on all the fullness God has for you.

So if you've ever wondered, "Is this really as good as it gets?" ... the answer is *no.*

Don't settle for complacently accepting your life as it is now. God has more available for you!

Is This Request a Good Request?

Should we pray for blessing?

Such a strong demand for blessing!

But is this prayer a good prayer to pray?

On the one hand, this prayer is amazing!

It's so specific!

It's so tangible!

It has such a focus on *results*.

On the other hand ... this prayer feels more than a little awkward.

Is it okay to ask God for blessing for ourselves?

Isn't that *greedy*?

Besides ... didn't Jesus say, "Foxes have dens and birds have nests, but the Son of Man has no place to lay his head"?

Shouldn't we be aiming for minimalism, poverty, and smallness?

The Greedy Prayer

On earth as it is in heaven

Is heaven a place of plenty or of poverty?

Think of the streets: are they paved with gold or riddled with potholes?

From heaven to earth: what environment makes you feel more safe, peaceful, and joyful: a well-tended public garden or a back alley in the inner city?

Jesus taught us to ask, "Thy kingdom come, thy will be done, on earth as it is in heaven."

Heaven is a place of plenty.

Let's bring that to earth.

Let's not seek to increase poverty.

Let's ask for the Lord to bless us instead.

But ... what about Jesus?

Good question.

Yes, Jesus didn't have a home base for ministry ... but this world was not actually his home.

He could multiply food, pay taxes with money found in a fish's mouth, and create wine from water.

Hardly impoverished with no resources at his disposal.

In Jesus' itinerant ministry, yes, many of his disciples were fishermen.

But he was also welcome among the wealthy, and had enough financial resources that he needed a treasurer.

At the time of his death, he was wearing a garment fine enough that the soldiers gambled to win it. (Perhaps the first century equivalent of a Versace suit?)

At the very least ... let's acknowledge that Jesus was not a typical homeless man, and he didn't celebrate poverty.

Seek for Glory

You have not because you ask not

Romans 2:7 says "To those who by perseverance in doing good seek glory, honor, and immortality, He will give eternal life."

If you persevere in well doing, you are seeking glory, honor, and immortality. You are meant for amazing and glorious things! Go for it and don't hold back!

Before Bob and I started to work together, my family's business hired Bob to pray, and we saw noticeable almost immediately.

My mom realized that, for 30 years, she and her staff had been praying for her customers, praying for her vendors, praying for the children, praying for the staff. But she said, "I never once asked for increase. I didn't even think about it."

On the other hand, Bob, as a paid intercessor, had no problem crying out for increase. He took very literally what the book of James says: "You have not because you ask not."[8]

When I partnered with him, I entered in to the weight of the intense, personal motivation. *If God doesn't show up, we have no business model.*

But the reward is that we get to have the excitement and the passion and the glory of praying for big requests and seeing God move in power in beautiful ways.

We happily pray for the bigger and better things that the business owners might be afraid to ask for.

We invite you, too, to seek for glory.

On Bold Prayers

Voice the desires of your heart

I was once talking to a friend about some of his goals and dreams. I enjoyed the conversation, full of so much big picture thinking.

Suddenly he said, "Is it okay if I pray for these things? Can I actually just say what I want? I don't know if I've ever voiced these desires of my heart. It's almost scary to speak them aloud."

In the months that followed, I heard this same hesitation expressed in a few other ways.

"I don't know if I should say what I really want. I don't want to appear proud."

"I have a specific request, but I'm not sure I should ask, because I don't know if I'm philanthropic enough. Maybe I want it just for me, and not for the wider world, so that might not be godly enough."

So ... should you restrict your ask, so as not to appear power-hungry, proud, or greedy?

Well ... Jabez asked for blessing and influence, for help and protection.

He prayed a big prayer, an uncommonly big prayer.

And he was more honorable than his brothers.

So we encourage you: voice the desires of your heart, even the largest ones.

You have permission to actually just say, "This is what I want."

The scripture says, "You have not because you ask not."
Jabez *asked*.

Look at what else the scripture says: "Now to Him who
is able to [carry out His purpose and] do superabundantly
more than all that we dare ask or think [infinitely beyond our
greatest prayers, hopes, or dreams], according to His power
that is at work within us."[9]

You can trust that the Lord will do more than what you ask,
think, or imagine.

But you have to be bold enough to ask.

You have the opportunity to come to the Lord, asking for
this Jabez blessing.

Pray big requests.

The New Testament Weighs In

The source of our desires

Still not convinced?

In Philippians 2:13, we read "For God is working in you, giving you the desire and the power to do what pleases him."[10]

Basically, because God works in us, his Spirit creates our desires as we walk with him.

As such, we can embrace the things that God has put on our hearts, because he gave us the desire to begin with.

And if we have a desire that isn't God-given?

We can pray, as Epaphras did for the church at Colossae, "that ye may stand perfect and complete in all the will of God."[11]

God is able to prune our desires as needed.

So *ask*!

Jesus and the Ten Lepers

What this story shows about blessings

Want an example of how coming to Jesus repeatedly results in more blessing?

Here is a famous story, with the truth obscured in translation.

In Luke 17:11-19, we read the story of the ten lepers who asked Jesus to heal them.

And as he entered a village, he was met by ten lepers, who stood at a distance and lifted up their voices and said, "Jesus, Master, have mercy on us." When he saw them he said to them, "Go and show yourselves to the priests." And as they went they were cleansed. Then one of them, when he saw that he was **healed***, turned back, praising God with a loud voice; and he fell on his face at Jesus' feet, giving him thanks. Now he was a Samaritan. Then said Jesus, "Were not ten cleansed? Where are the nine? Was no one found to return and give praise to God except this foreigner?" And he said to him, "Rise and go your way; your faith* **has made you well***."*

The words *healed* and *made you well* are not the same word.

When the leper saw that he was healed—the word here means *physical healing*—he returned to thank Jesus.

But when Jesus blessed him at the end of this story, when the man was *made well*, Jesus spoke the verb *sozo*.

The Greek uses different words for *saved* (the gift of salvation), *healed* (physical healing), and *delivered* (deliverance from evil spirits).

But *sozo* means all three: saved, healed, and delivered.

So that leper wasn't just *healed* of his leprosy. He was also *saved* (made right with God) and *delivered* (freed from evil spirits).

All ten people with leprosy received physical healing.

But the tenth, the man who returned to Jesus, received more than physical healing.

He received all that Jesus had to offer.

Get close to God.

He always has more for you.

He always has more for you.

Can you hear the pounding on the table?

Don't be complacent!

Get all that God has!

Ask for blessings!

How to Ask with Boldness

Because God loves you, too

Even if you find it hard to ask for large requests for yourself, can you ask for someone else?

One of my friends, during healing prayer, was asked to close the door on obsessive eating.

She resisted ... until suddenly she realized that she might pass her own food dysfunction down to her daughter.

As soon as she realized that, she slammed the door shut and locked it. "I am not passing this on to my daughter!"

Similarly with parents who tend toward a minimal lifestyle. Even if they don't want to be wealthy, they (usually) don't want their children to be impoverished, to be struggling with money.

So it's much easier to ask for people you love: "Bless them!"

Does it still feel awkward to ask for that for yourself? Does it feel greedy?

Probably so! Most of us aren't used to praying blessings over ourselves!

Perhaps part of the journey with God is to say, "Teach me to ask in faith that what you do for other people you'll do for me as well, and that I am not disadvantaged in any way. Thank you that you love me, too."

One Final Thought About Blessings

Thy kingdom come

We know from Romans 14:17 that God's kingdom is righteousness, peace, and joy in the Holy Spirit.

We know from Psalms 37:25 that the steps of the righteous are ordered by the Lord.

So as we're praying, "Oh, God, bless me indeed," we're also praying, "thy kingdom come."

We are saying, "Oh, God, establish your kingdom in my life. Let your kingdom come, your will be done, on earth as it is in heaven. We pray that for ourselves and our family and loved ones."

Pray the Blessing

From the first request

Lord, bring increase, increase, increase, increase.

Any way you want, Lord, but please bring it.

May we not settle for what we've had before, nor assume that what happened before will happen again.

May we break free from any spirit of foreboding, and instead look ahead with joy for what you are about to do.

Let us put no limits on you, Lord. Let us not give in to apathy.

Lord, we pray that the Spirit of the Lord will be upon us, and that we would cry out in the midst of our circumstances and situations: oh, God, bless us, indeed.

And Lord, that "indeed" means, "let us be lavished with the blessings of our king."

Lord, as your royal priesthood, would you give us gifts, unexpected gifts?

Would you grant us favor? Unexpected increase of favor?

Would you give us more authority?

Would you give us more revelation in our identity in Christ and of Christ?

And Lord, would you release more of your charisma in us, the anointing of God, the favor of God, the wisdom, knowledge, understanding, and discernment of the Lord?

Would you increase the power voltage in us to see people healed, to see people set free?

Would you also increase the power of God that releases the

ability to make wealth and bring in finances and resources?
Generate favor in every area of our lives!
Thank you, Lord!

THE SECOND REQUEST

Another Big Ask

And enlarge my territory!

Expand
Extend
Enlarge

My territory
My border
My coast
My property

Give me

A lot
Much
More

Land

You have made my border great.

Prayer for Expanded Borders

Metaphorical possibilities

It's possible that you want more land and a larger house, so that your prayer here becomes, "I need more acreage and square feet!"

But this doesn't need to be a literal request.

Metaphorically, we could pray this, meaning, "Enlarge my influence and impact."

For Bob, serving in Latvia, he prayed this request that he might live large for God.

He cried out for the touch of greatness in his life.

He cried out for a rich legacy, a legacy that would grow, and last for multiple generations.

What enlarged borders do you want?

More effectiveness in raising up your children, so that when you release them, they are arrows that hit the bullseye?

An expanded ministry?

Greater success at work, so that you can touch additional lives?

Or perhaps you're seeking your purpose?

Whatever would make you feel like you are expanding.

Literal Requests Are Good, Too

Possibilities abound

Though this doesn't have to be a literal request, you can actually make it a literal request.

Some possibilities to pray for:

- **Fame**: "Do you see someone skilled in their work? They will serve before kings; they will not serve before officials of low rank."[12]
- **Favor**: "For those who find me find life and receive favor from the Lord."[13]
- **Promotion**: "Whoever pursues righteousness and love finds life, prosperity and honor."[14]
- **Stocks to increase in value**: "I form the light and create darkness, I bring prosperity and create disaster; I, the Lord, do all these things."[15]
- **Wells and oil rights to multiply**: "I will give you hidden treasures, riches stored in secret places, so that you may know that I am the Lord, the God of Israel, who summons you by name."[16]
- **Gold, silver, gems and precious stones**: "And I will make the Egyptians favorably disposed toward this people, so that when you leave you will not go empty-handed. Every woman is to ask her neighbor and any woman living in her house for articles of silver and gold and for clothing, which you will put on your sons and daughters. And so you will plunder the Egyptians."[17]

- **Company greatness**: "From the fruit of their lips people are filled with good things, and the work of their hands brings them reward."[18]
- **Community value to go up**: "Also, seek the peace and prosperity of the city to which I have carried you into exile. Pray to the Lord for it, because if it prospers, you too will prosper."[19]

In partnership with the Holy Spirit, what do you want to request?

As we are in partnership with God, he gives us desires, then sanctifies those desires, and finally satisfies them, too.

When we have the desire to pray for something, we get to do so in partnership with God. Our desires, as the Lord's covenant people, come about because of the Lord's will. We wonder if maybe we create those desires, but, no ... the Holy Spirit is at work.

We're in collaboration with God.

Why God Blesses

Not for us alone

When God spoke to Abram, he called him out of his homeland, promising him:

"I will make you into a great nation,
and I will bless you;
I will make your name great,
and you will be a blessing.
I will bless those who bless you,
and whoever curses you I will curse;
and all peoples on earth
will be blessed through you."[20]

Did you catch that? When God blessed Abraham, it wasn't so that he could keep all the blessing for himself!

He blessed him to bless others!

So as the Lord blesses you and increases your influence and impact, you then get to be the conduit of blessing to those around you!

What a privilege!

Be Ready Always

Imitate Christ

The record of the New Testament shows that, when people encountered Jesus or his followers, and they entered into the kingdom of God, they imitated what they had seen.

- Jesus spoke healing to the rejected Samaritan woman at the well, and she led her entire region to him.
- Jesus delivered the man with a legion of demons, and that man stayed in his region, telling all that the Lord had done for him. When Jesus returned, the region was ready to hear.
- A paralyzed man, after Jesus heals him, gets a bit saucy with the religious leaders: stop bullying me, because you can't do what he did!
- Philemon, when he received back his escaped slave Onesimus, got to choose to extend the kingdom to him. (Which he presumably did, as there is an Onesimus, bishop of Ephesus, in the historical record.)

This is part of extending your influence: imitate Jesus and pass on what is given to you.

- If you had a spirit of death broken off of you, break it off of others, as soon as you identify it.
- If you were healed physically, pray for others, that they, too, may be healed.
- If you found your voice, pray that others find their voices, too.
- If you have had a financial reversal from poverty to wealth, pray that God would do the same for others.

As part of the abundant life that God promises, we share his life with those around us.

Hallelujah!

Pray the Increase

From the second request

Lord God, as we have prayed for your blessing, would you also bring an increase of influence?

Would you enlarge our impact?

Would you increase our borders?

Would you increase our authority and dominion?

Would you increase our resources?

Would you increase our ministry?

Lord God, your word says in Hosea 4:6, "My people are destroyed from lack of knowledge."

Lord, in some ways the ease of actual turnaround in people's lives through prayer is *so easy.*

And yet we don't know how to do it, and so we're stuck praying insipid, faithless prayers, *because we don't know any better.*

We are crying out, Lord, that the destruction stops.

That your people will stop the narrative that is hopeless, day after day, year after year, plodding forward until death, faithfulness but without a whole lot of joy or hope.

We long for that narrative to end.

We long for that weariness and heaviness to be broken off, and that your people would walk free in the abundant life that you, Jesus, promise.

We want an increase of you in our lives!

An increase of world change!

An increase of your kingdom!

We cry out for it, pounding on the table, desperate for you to break in!

THE THIRD REQUEST

Because This Will Be Necessary

Let your hand be with me

Please be with me in all that I do
Be with me
May your power be with me
Keep your power with me
Your hand has been with me

The Hand of the LORD

Because this will be necessary

In the scripture, we find *"the hand of God"* and *"the hand of the LORD,"* also variations like *"the arm of the LORD"* and *"the Lord's hand."*

In the Old Testament, the hand of the LORD would deliver the Israelites, which meant that that same hand would be against their enemies.

For example, in Joshua 4:24, scripture says, that God piled up the waters of the Jordan and allowed the children of Israel to cross over, "So that all the peoples of the earth might know that the hand of the Lord is powerful and so that you might always fear the Lord your God."[21]

In the New Testament, we also see God's hand, as in Acts 11:21: "The Lord's hand was with them [early Jesus followers], and a great number of people [in Antioch] believed and turned to the Lord."[22]

We want the hand of the Lord in our lives, to come and save and deliver, to move in power.

And we celebrate the beautiful promise in Isaiah 49:15-16: "Can a mother forget the baby at her breast and have no compassion on the child she has borne? Though she may forget, I will not forget you! See, I have engraved you on the palms of my hands...."[23]

We have not only been placed in God's hands, but our names have been inscribed in them.

The Hand of God

Several possible graces

Jesus, in the Lord's prayer, called God, "Our Father."[24]
Think of the tasks that a loving parent's hands do, in rough
chronological order.

- **Tender Care**: diaper changes, carrying from place to
  place, protecting from harm, clothing and caressing.
- **Protect**: My mother told the story of biking with me as a
  baby (apparently back when holding a baby while biking
  was still a thing), when somehow she crashed her bike. "I
  landed on my elbow, but I was glad to see that I protected
  you instinctively."
- **Feed**: think of a parent, offering first bites of food to a
  young child.
- **Correct**: redirect in a variety of ways, in order to help
  train a child to proper behavior.
- **Connect**: how much children love to hold the hands of
  their loving parent!
- **Play**: two parents swing a young child between them. A
  child and a parent play a board game, or a game of catch.
- **Teach, Instruct, Mentor**: demonstrate how to do things.
  Tie a shoe, build a fire, aim a BB gun, cook an egg, play
  solitaire, read and write ... the list goes on.
- **Encourage**: a tired child on the trail gets a gentle hand on
  the back to provide a little extra power. A hand on the
  shoulder to gently guide.

- **Applaud**: clap and fist pump and throw in the air to cele-brate successes.

So when you ask for God's hand to be with you, you are asking for provision and protection, for God to encourage and instruct you.

Further Along

These requests build

We ask for blessing, and God provides.
We ask for an increase of influence, and God answers.
Then the bewilderment sets in.
How to manage, to handle, this increase?
How to deal with the overwhelm?
Help!
We ask for the hand of God to be with us.
I once heard Rabbi Daniel Lapin teach on the third day of creation. He emphasized the word *mikvah*, meaning, *the collection of water* or *the gathering*, which comes from the same root as the word *hope*.

Because water represents life and hope.

Rabbi Lapin then said that *mikvah* is used with the Hebrew word *taume*, a word usually translated *impure* or *unclean*. But neither of those are good translations.

The concept of *taume* doesn't exist in English, at least not exactly, but it's the subconscious sense of being overwhelmed by a feeling or atmosphere of death.

You might think of a feeling of being suppressed or unhappy.

How fascinating, that the Hebrew has a word for this feeling that we've all experienced: overwhelm, dread, hopelessness.

And the Lord has a solution: cleansing with water.

Hope.

Jesus said, "The thief comes only to steal and kill and destroy; I have come that they may have life, and have it to the full."[25]

Amen and amen!

God's Hand Gives Wisdom

A guaranteed prayer

Do you cry out for wisdom multiple times a day?

How blessed we are to accept the promise of James 1:5: "If any of you lacks wisdom, you should ask God, who gives generously to all without finding fault, and it will be given to you."

And how delightful, the description of different facets of God's wisdom in Isaiah 11:2: "The Spirit of the Lord will rest on him—the Spirit of wisdom and of understanding, the Spirit of counsel and of might, the Spirit of the knowledge and fear of the Lord."

This same verse in the New English Translation says, "The Lord's Spirit will rest on him—a Spirit that gives extraordinary wisdom, a Spirit that provides the ability to execute plans, a Spirit that produces absolute loyalty to the Lord."

Are you desperate for extraordinary wisdom?

Desperate for the ability to execute plans?

We need God's strength and strategy.

Let's cry out for wisdom to be able to accomplish the different tasks that the Lord has put in our hands to do.

He sends us the wisdom we need.

Dependence

God gives us help

At one point, I was seeking to launch a ministry. A mentor said to me, "Expect to feel over your head all the time from now on. That's part of the walk of faith."

Ah. An opportunity to daily put into practice Paul's words to the Corinthian church: "But he said to me, 'My grace is sufficient for you, for my power is made perfect in weakness.' Therefore I will boast all the more gladly about my weaknesses, so that Christ's power may rest on me."[26]

God's power, made perfect in *weakness*, not in strength.

I was fascinated, then, to find an almost identical story in Bruce Wilkinson's book *The Prayer of Jabez*. Bruce told of how God answered his prayers for blessing and increase.

And he soon felt completely out of his depth.

He went to speak to John Mitchell, a trusted counselor and Bible teacher, explaining how he was pretty sure he wasn't the right man for the job.

"'Son,' [Mitchell] said, in his kindly brogue, 'that feeling you are running from is called dependence. It means you're walking with the Lord Jesus.' He paused to let me take in his word, then continued. 'Actually, the second you're not feeling dependent is the second you've backed away from truly living by faith'."[27]

In short, that unsettled feeling was the evidence that Wilkinson was on the *right* path, not the wrong one.

"It's a frightening and utterly exhilarating truth, isn't it? As God's chosen, blessed sons and daughters, we are expected to attempt something large enough that failure is guaranteed ... unless God steps in."[28]

For the independent, the reasonably competent, or those who seek to be comfortable—this is not exactly welcome news.

Oh, Lord, teach us your ways! May we rest in the reassurance of Zechariah 4:6, where the word of the LORD says, "Not by might nor by power, but by my Spirit."

Pray the Help

From the third request

Lord, we thank you that the hand of God is upon us.

"Thy kingdom come, thy will be done in our lives, in our work, in our ministry, in our business, in our enterprises, in our families."

Thy kingdom come.

Oh Lord, may your anointing flow through us. May your Holy Spirit be close. May the finger of God precisely operate through us. Amen.

THE FOURTH REQUEST

Because Advance Comes with Risk

And keep me from harm so that
I will be free from pain

Of the four requests, this is the most variable in translation.

Keep me from all trouble and pain!

Keep me from harm:
So that it might not bring me pain!
So that *it* would not hurt me!
So I might not endure pain!
So that I will not experience pain.

So I will be safe from harm.
Keep me from anything evil that might cause me pain.
Keep me from evil, and keep me from harm!
Save me from being oppressed by evil.

Keep *me* from evil:
That it may not grieve me!
That it may not pain me!
That it does not hurt me!
That it be not to my sorrow!

One plaintive request, that implies more a need for
emotional support than deliverance:
Make me know that thou wilt not grieve me!

And two translations that are more outward focused, on the wider community.

Keep me from harm, so that I will not cause any pain.

Keep me from evil, that I may not cause pain!

And Keep Me

From harm

The Hebrew *rah*, "harm," defined.

Bad
Evil
Disagreeable
Malignant
Unpleasant
Giving pain
Unhappiness
Misery
Displeasing
Displeasure
Worse than
Worst
Sad
Unhappy
Hurt
Hurtful
Unkind
Vicious in disposition
Wicked
Wickedness
Distress
Injury
Calamity

Adversity
Wrong
Mischief
Trouble
Sore
Affliction
Ill
Ill-favored
Harm
Naught
Noisome
Grievous
Grief
Heavy
Sorrow
Vex
Wretchedness

Yes, keep all far from us.

That I May Be Free

From pain

The Hebrew *asab*, "pain," defined.

Hurt
Pain
Grieve
Displease
Vex
Wrest
Torture
Sorry
Cause pain

Yes, let us be free from these.

So Much Pain

So that I will be free from pain

Because of the range of meanings in the various translations, let's look at some of the possibilities of the final request of Jabez.

Though keep in mind that, as with good poetry, he is not asking for only one of these categories. Rather, his request actually includes all of these shades of meaning.

1. Keep me from bad situations.

The first category of request, including words like *harm, pain, trouble*, sounds more like a desire for protection from bad circumstances.

Keep me from sickness, from financial loss, from drama, from accidents. Don't let a wildfire sweep through my area and destroy my property.

2. Keep me from evil.

The second category is more like targeted malicious attack.

I don't want the grief from being targeted! I don't want the pain, the hurt, the sorrow, knowing that enemies seek my downfall.

Keep me from demonic oppression.

Keep me from evil men who seek my hurt.

Don't let an arsonist come to torch my house while me and my family are sleeping.

3. Remind me of who you are.

The Brenton Septuagint Translation says, "Make me know
that thou wilt not grieve me!"

This request cries out for a clarification of God's identity.

God, do you cause pain?

Do you destroy? Or is that the enemy?

Are you for me? Or against me?

(In case you're not sure of the answer to these questions,
remember that Jesus gave a clear answer about who was for
us, and who against us: "The thief comes only in order to steal
and kill and destroy. I came that they may have and enjoy life,
and have it in abundance [to the full, till it overflows]."[29])

4. Don't let me become a menace.

The Holman Christian Standard Bible translates this
request as, "Keep me from harm, so that I will not cause
any pain."

The New King James Version is similar: "Keep *me* from evil,
that I may not cause pain!"

What's the popular saying? "Hurt people hurt people."

How particularly poignant for Jabez, whose mother bore
him in pain, and so gave him a name as a curse.

You can hear him voicing this request: "My mother entered
into pain, and that caused me pain. But now keep that pain
far from me, because I want to treat those around me with
greater gentleness and grace. Let me not be a vector of pain."

The Strategic Problem of Advancing

More directions of attack

When you study trench warfare during World War I, whenever one side would advance into enemy territory, they created a bulge in their line, a peninsula of advance.

And so, instead of facing attack from only one direction, now they had to fend off attacks in three directions.

Terrible.

As you advance, then, your protection becomes even more important, because the number of ways that you can fail increase exponentially.

Ever wonder why it seems like so many godly leaders fail?

This is a strong possibility: because they advance, and the pressure increases enormously.

Ask to Avoid the Fight

Easier to avoid than endure

At the end of the Lord's prayer, Jesus said, "Lead us not into temptation, but deliver us from evil."[30]

Or, in a more modern translation: "And lead us not into temptation, but deliver us from the evil one."[31]

In either case, notice that Jesus doesn't say, "Deliver us *through* evil."

He says, "Deliver us *from* evil."

It's like saying, "Don't make me go *through* the storm. Keep the storm away from me."

Why would we choose to be in a battle, rather than avoid it altogether?

How much easier to simply not face the attack!

Don't seek to endure.

Rather, ask to avoid.

We get to ask God to protect us from attacks, rather than pray for the ability to withstand. Because, all things considered, we're actually pretty bad at avoiding attacks.

As Bruce Wilkinson points out: "Adam and Eve weren't any more prone to succumb to temptation than we are. In fact, unlike us, they were perfect in every way, and none of their genuine needs were unmet. Satan approached the human race at its peak of promise and performance—and crushed us with one friendly conversation."[32]

Better to avoid a fight than to trade blows.

Ask God to allow you to simply avoid the attack.

Pray the Protection

From the fourth request

Lord, Jabez said, "Deliver me from pain."

Oh, Lord, you prayed, "Lead us from temptation and deliver us from evil."

Lord, keep us from trouble. Lead us from temptation. Keep us from pain.

Lord, we ask you for your protection. Your word says that you are a refuge and a fortress.[33]

"Our help is in the name of the LORD."[34]

And so, Lord, we see life as full of obstacles, and bumps and bruises that lead to disappointment and pain.

Lord, would you protect us? Would you shield us from the enemy's threats? Would you shield us from the enemy's curses? Would you shield us from the enemy's storms that would cause pain and wreak havoc?

Lord Jesus, be the shield about us. Deliver us from pain and keep us from evil. Surround us. Keep us from trouble.

We ask for heaven's resources, the angelic host, to fight on our behalf.

Lord, keep us from decisions that we would make that might not be the right decisions, or might not be in the right sequence or the right timing. We seek your face.

May the Spirit of the Lord rest upon us, and grant us the grace and peace found in Christ.

And we think of your name, Holy Spirit, as the Comforter. We think of how, when Jesus told his disciples about his future, they were alarmed, concerned, and didn't want to accept it.

But Jesus, you said, "No, it's to your advantage that I leave and the Holy Spirit comes. He will be your Comforter."[35]

And so we're asking, Lord, that in the midst of any pain, that you bring comfort. In the midst of disappointment, that you bring hope. In the season of darkness, or, as Psalm 23 calls it, the valley of the shadow—when things don't work, prayers don't seem to be answered, hardship remains and disappointment prevails, your word says that you will be with us in those painful moments.

ADDITIONAL THOUGHTS

Granted

And God granted his request

After all these big requests, look at the sentence after the prayer ends. It doesn't say, "And God, angered, smote Jabez for asking for too many blessings."

No.

Jabez prayed a big prayer.

"And God *granted* his request."

God said yes.

And God

granted
brought about

what he asked.
what he requested.
the things he prayed for.

God brings in that which he asked.
God answered his prayer.
And God did just what Jabez had asked.

And God granted him all that he asked.

Not a Formula

How to pray repeatedly and not get bored

This prayer is not a formula or a mantra.

How, though, do we avoid a sense of the formulaic as we pray?

And, yes, every day we're praying anew, because every day is new, never been lived before.

But no matter what template we use, it can become dry and boring.

Bob has been praying this prayer and the Lord's prayer for decades. So how has he managed to keep from getting stale?

Romans 14:23 says that "everything that does not come from faith is sin," so living from faith is clearly vitally important.

But this isn't done with willpower, our power, grit prayer.

Instead, we get to ask the Holy Spirit for fresh inspiration. Lean on the Lord: *Holy Spirit. Help me. I don't want to get in a rut. Give me faith. I don't want to rely on discipline or character alone, but on faith and hope.*

When we make this request, we have faith that God is near, and God will respond, and God will reward. These prayers need to be alive.

And then, from the place of faith-filled, living prayer, then we persevere. If we don't want to pray, we admit, *Holy Spirit, I don't feel like praying today. I need help.*

And then we pray, despite how we feel. We endure and press in, recognizing that these words are not the spiritual equivalent of a gumball machine, where we put in a prayer and get out a result. These prayers aren't positive words to give you a squirt of happy juice.

Rather, prayer creates connection and relationship. As you pray, you nurture your connection with the God who wants to help you, who wants you to succeed, who wants you to thrive.

Pray for Others

Give a gift to those you love

You don't have to just pray the prayer of Jabez only over your own life!

You can use this prayer for others, too, by position (my family; my mentors and teachers; my colleagues), and by name.

Here's an example:

Oh, Lord, would you bless my family indeed today. Show them that you're Jehovah-jireh, the God who provides. Show them that you're Jehovah-shalom, the God of peace. Show them that you're Jehovah-nissi, God our banner, in Jesus' name.

Would you direct their steps, Lord God? Would you enlarge their influence, bring an increase, bring impact?

Lord, give them all that they need to accomplish all that you have for them this day. May your hand be on them, to help and protect.

And, Lord, please watch over them. Keep them hidden in you. May they not fight any battles they don't need to fight. Keep evil far from them.

Thank you, Lord, that you honor these requests. You're a good God.

A Variation of the Full Prayer

An example of how to expand on the structure

Lord God, we thank you for the example of Jabez, that he was more honorable than his brothers. Lord, he was an example of someone who wasn't content with the status quo, who sought for more, and who had a passion to see change come to his generation.

Lord, we thank you that in the midst of hundreds of names, that he was a standout, and that you honored his request.

Lord, as he asked, "Oh, Lord, bless me, indeed," thank you that he wasn't embarrassed by the request, that he longed for more of you so much, that he didn't have a religious spirit that would say, "Oh, don't extend yourself too much. Don't be too proud."

Thank you that he saw that you were a big God, that you offered big rewards, that you were the same God who brought the children of Israel out of Egypt, and gave them all that they asked for, that they really plundered the Egyptians as they left. These people who had been their overlords for so long, then were so happy that the Israelites were leaving after the ten plagues, that they gave them riches as they left.

Lord, Jabez knew that you were that good.

Thank you, Lord, for his request. Thank you.

And then Lord, as he said, "Enlarge my influence," we cry out for that, too. We want your kingdom-minded people to be the ones who have influence in this world, Lord God.

We recognize that you are able to act supernaturally, that

you are able to create the connections that we need, to give the visions that we need, to bring those visions to fruition.

Lord, thank you that you are the one who acts in the midst of our day-to-day, that you reach down and create the connections that we need, that you are able to propel us to the places where we need to be.

And Lord, thank you that we do not have to be under *Kronos* time. We don't have to strive. You are a God who is able to do multiplication without striving, you are the one who is able to create beautiful situations, beautiful opportunities, at the right time. You live in the fullness of time, the *Kairos* time. Thank you for that. Thank you, Lord, that you enlarge our influence in your time.

Then, Lord, thank you that you are able to perform that which you call us to do. Lord, as we ask for more, you give us more, but you also give us the opportunity to be dependent on you.

You say that your strength is made perfect in our weakness. And so it's not that we need to somehow become superheroes or incredibly strong people, but you work through us as we depend on you.

And so, Lord, we ask that your hand would be on us, your hand of protection and your hand of provision, your hand of encouragement and your hand of blessing. Lord, that the finger of God would be on us, that we would bear your fingerprint, that we would bear your imprint in this world.

Lord God, thank you.

And then, Lord God, we ask that you would keep us from the evil one. May we live in the secret place that is so secret that the enemy cannot even find us.

And, Lord, as we abide in that place, as we abide in the vine, thank you that the enemy is defeated. Thank you that we don't have to go through life in this constant battle, but that we can live hidden in you.

Lord, thank you that this prayer, which seems in many

ways to be an overreaching prayer, is actually just a confident prayer in your goodness.

Thank you, Lord, that the record of this scripture is that you answered this request. And so we ask that you would do it again in our generation.

Do it again, Lord God, do it again.

Thank you.

In your precious and holy name, Jesus, amen.

The Challenge of Subtle Effects

One reason it's good to take notes

One of my friends told me this story.

My husband went to a big box store once, and he was so irritated by how difficult it was to find certain foods, he said he would never go again.

That was years ago.

He's been doing healing prayer recently, and one day he called me up and said, "Hey, do you need anything from the big box store? I'm in the area, and I could run in and do the shopping."

This has never happened before.

But when I pointed out to him that this must be an effect of healing prayer, he said, "Oh, no. I was just in the area."

But he's been in that area probably hundreds of times, and never once thought to do the shopping before healing prayer.

This is one difficulty of prayer. Sometimes the results are shockingly amazing.

Sometimes they are so subtle, they are easy to miss.

At one point in his life, Bob prayed over the Final Four March Madness Tournament. College basketball coaches track *everything*. They know their statistics.

They could track that, with prayer, the tournament had fewer injuries. The coaches had fewer divorces. The arenas had fewer issues with brawls.

The outcome of the tournament was not the focus of the prayer, but rather the peace of God on the entire event.

But these are subtle shifts, not evident except to those with eyes to see.

We would like to encourage you, then, to take notes.

Over the next month, pray this prayer.

Note any changes in your life. Even small ones.

Because small changes can grow to become large.

A Blessing to Close

You are sent out

Lord, we thank you for the beautiful prayer of Numbers 6, the blessing of God, given to Moses, the government leader, who then gave to his brother Aaron, the priestly leader.

We see Aaron, the priest and intercessor, valued.

Aaron spoke this blessing. And, as intercessors, we speak this blessing over you.[36]

The Lord bless you, and keep you [protect you, sustain you, and guard you];

The Lord make His face shine upon you [with favor],

And be gracious to you [surrounding you with lovingkindness];

The Lord lift up His countenance (face) upon you [with divine approval],

And give you peace [a tranquil heart and life].

NOTES

1 Genesis 22:14
2 Exodus 17:15
3 Judges 6:23-24
4 Jeremiah 23:5-6
5 Jeremiah 33:14-16
6 Ezekiel 48:35b
7 For the four requests, Amy took 26 different translations of the scripture and combined them, to suss out the different variations of meaning.
8 James 4:2
9 Ephesians 3:20 AMP
10 New Living Translation
11 Colossians 4:12
12 Proverbs 22:29
13 Proverbs 8:35
14 Proverbs 21:21
15 Isaiah 45:7
16 Isaiah 45:3
17 Exodus 3:21-22
18 Proverbs 12:14
19 Jeremiah 29:7
20 Genesis 12:2-3
21 Joshua 4:24
22 Acts 11:21
23 Isaiah 49:15-16
24 Matthew 6:9
25 John 10:10
26 II Corinthians 12:9
27 Wilkinson, Bruce. The Prayer of Jabez. New York: Penguin Random House, 2000, p. 47.
28 Ibid.
29 John 10:10 AMP
30 Matthew 6:13 KJV
31 New International Version
32 Wilkinson, Bruce. The Prayer of Jabez. New York: Penguin Random House, 2000, p. 69.
33 Psalm 91:2
34 Psalm 124:8
35 Paraphrase of John 16:7
36 Numbers 6:24-26 (AMP)

ABOUT THE AUTHORS

Bob Perry has been a passionate student of prayer for more than four decades, constantly asking, "Lord, teach me to pray." He has founded and led multiple prayer initiatives that have trained and mobilized hundreds of thousands of people in prayer partnerships.

Amy Joy Lykosh loves healing and deliverance. Her heart's cry comes from the verse, "My people are destroyed for lack of knowledge" (Hosea 4:6). The author of several highly acclaimed books, she seeks to stop the destruction as best she can through writing and speaking.

Together, they run Workplace Prayer, to cover businesses in prayer, and Prayer Mentoring, to raise up healthy intercessors to bring the kingdom of God to bear in their lives and communities.

MAKARIOS
PRESS

Be in your happy place.

AS IT IS IN HEAVEN
Why Workplace Prayer Exists

When Jesus taught on prayer, he began, "Our Father in heaven, hallowed be your name, your kingdom come, your will be done, on earth as it is in heaven." How can we effectively pray God's kingdom on earth, if we don't know what heaven looks like? If we want to pray better, we need to understand what we're praying for. Catch a glimpse of heaven in these short free verse poems, taken from Revelation 4 and 5. Pressed for time? You could read a single chapter. Or even a single poem!

> "I just sat down with your book. I am on the second page. In tears. Thank you. Beautiful and song-like. And fun." — **Sarah**

> "I feel like each line of each poem is like a choice morsel of truth that I just want to savor slowly. I set aside your book to read in quiet and cozy moments wrapped in a quilt on my bed. It is something I look forward to and cherish." — **Elena**

> "I love the short meditative chapters. It's great bedtime reading. Congratulations!!" — **Perry Marshall**

FIND OUT MORE AT
makariospress.com/heaven

ORDER AT
amazon.com

THE PRINCE PROTECTS HIS CITY

Nehemiah Prayed Four Months, Then Rebuilt the Wall in Only 52 Days

Such a great story! But how easy to miss!

Nehemiah wasn't a warrior or a king. He was a tremendous administrator, a gifted leader, a world-class historian, a treasured friend, a successful fund-raiser, and a prince. Though he was never a CEO, he headed an enormous public works project he had planned, then served as governor for twelve years. And he prayed constantly. A free verse look at the book of Nehemiah. Come meet a man who brought God's kingdom to bear in his work.

> "I finished reading it today! Loved it. Such a nice quick pace to read Nehemiah and also space to sit in parts if I just wanted to read one page" — **Angela**

FIND OUT MORE AT
makariospress.com/the-prince-protects-his-city

ORDER AT
amazon.com

GROW WITH PRAYER EXPERIENCES

Throughout the year, we offer a wide range of prayer experiences: Communal Fasts, Prayer Challenges, and Sacred Assemblies.

If you want to grow in prayer in creative and unexpected ways, come join us.

FIND OUT MORE AT
PrayerExperiences.com

ONE VOICE: THE STORY OF WILLIAM WILBERFORCE

Gorgeous Story of Tenacity + Courage

Biography in verse of the man who, despite all obstacles, fought to end the Slave Trade in Great Britain. Powerful story of tenacity and courage.

> "I think it's important to know Wilberforce's story, but One Voice has become one of my absolute favourite books of all time and is SO worth buying just for the beautiful writing. I was so skeptical when I first opened it and realized it was written in free verse but oh, it's so, so special. I can't make it through without sobbing." — **Emily**

ORDER EXCLUSIVELY AT
sonlight.com

---

21 DAYS OF A F(E)AST

A Fast That Feels More Like a Feast

Why fasting is a joy, and why you should do it. A guide for a fast that anyone can do, even if you can't restrict calories. The four types of fasting, and how to choose. Morning and evening readings for 21 days. Stories and testimonies. Drawn from four decades of experience and wisdom. Come sit in the Lord's presence.

> "Appreciating the wealth within this book!! Such a brilliant resource!" — **Nicole**

ORDER AT
amazon.com

PRAYER REFRESH
Short Prayers to Pray Through Your Day

You don't have to completely change your life, your habits, your personality, or your social media usage in order to have a good prayer life.

This book introduces a wide variety of prayers that you can pray in a minute or less, that will fit into your day, right where you are. Don't start with hours on your knees. Start with the stray half minutes here and there. Use it as a devotional for 21 days, or read straight through.

> "The Prayer Refresh was so life changing, perspective shattering, and breathed so much, much needed life into me and our home that I long to go through it again. Regularly. Like monthly." — **Amanda**

JUNETEENTH: AN INVITATION TO FAST
Both the Why and the How To

Join us in a one-day fast.

> "The booklet was so helpful with the historical summary of the date (which I knew nothing about), as well as specific prayers and family examples, to guide my focused petitions. The format is beautiful, and so clearly organized! Great resource!" — **Eileen**